ABDO Publishing Company

BUGS!
Lice

Kristin Petrie

visit us at
www.abdopublishing.com

Published by ABDO Publishing Company, 8000 West 78th Street, Edina, Minnesota 55439.
Copyright © 2009 by Abdo Consulting Group, Inc. International copyrights reserved in all
countries. No part of this book may be reproduced in any form without written permission from the
publisher. The Checkerboard Library™ is a trademark and logo of ABDO Publishing Company.

Printed in the United States.

Cover Photo: Getty Images
Interior Photos: Alamy pp. 4, 8–9, 13, 17, 25; Animals Animals p. 5; Corbis p. 23; Getty Images
    pp. 1, 11, 26, 27; iStockphoto pp. 17, 22, 29; Peter Arnold pp. 16, 19, 20, 21, 24;
    Photo Researchers pp. 7, 10, 15, 28

Series Coordinator: BreAnn Rumsch
Editors: Megan M. Gunderson, BreAnn Rumsch
Art Direction & Cover Design: Neil Klinepier

Library of Congress Cataloging-in-Publication Data

Petrie, Kristin, 1970-
 Lice / Kristin Petrie.
    p. cm. -- (Bugs!)
 Includes index.
 ISBN 978-1-60453-070-4
 1. Lice--Juvenile literature. I. Title.

 QL540.P48 2008
 595.7'56--dc22

                    2008004793

Contents

Lurking Lice

What are the least favorite bugs in the world? Many people would agree that lice deserve this title. Nearly everyone knows what lice are, and they know they don't want them. Just say the word *lice* and people cringe, groan, and start scratching their heads.

Lice are very common. They flourish in schools and on animal farms. Whenever people, animals, or birds are close together, lice can crawl quickly between these hosts. This makes lice important **ectoparasites**.

Keep reading to learn more about this tiny, annoying insect. Your head may feel itchy while you do so! Don't worry, this is a normal reaction. If you think you may have lice, ask an adult to check. Knowing more may help you keep lice off your head!

There are almost 3,000 known louse species. Hopefully, none of them will end up on you!

What Are They?

Lice are insects. Like all insects, they are from the class Insecta. Within this class, lice belong to the order Phthiraptera. This name comes from words in the Greek language. The word *phthir* means "lice," and *aptera* means "wingless." Put them together and you have wingless lice.

Some **entomologists** divide Phthiraptera into two **suborders**. They are Mallophaga and Anoplura. The difference between these suborders is the type of mouthparts the lice have.

If a louse bites, it has jaws and is from the suborder Mallophaga. Chewing lice **infest** birds and mammals. If a louse has stylets used for sucking, it is from the suborder Anoplura. Sucking lice are the only lice that infest humans. Head, body, and crab lice are all human lice.

Each species of louse has a two-word name called a binomial. A binomial combines the genus with a descriptive name, or epithet. For example, a chicken body louse's binomial is *Menacanthus stramineus.*

BUG BYTES

Chewing lice are ten times more abundant than sucking lice.

THAT'S CLASSIFIED!

Scientists use a method called scientific classification to sort the world's living organisms into groups. Eight groups make up the basic classification system. In descending order, they are domain, kingdom, phylum, class, order, family, genus, and species.

The phrase "Dear King Philip, come out for goodness' sake!" may help you remember this order. The first letter of each word is a clue for each group.

Domain is the most basic group. Species is the most specific group. Members of a species share common characteristics. Yet, they are different from all other living things in at least one way.

Body Parts

Despite their different mouthparts, chewing and sucking lice have similar bodies. Like all insects, they have three body **segments**. These are the head, the thorax, and the abdomen.

ABDOMEN

Lice also have six legs and an exoskeleton. The exoskeleton is a stiff outer covering that is much like a shell. It gives lice their shape and protects their insides.

In addition, the exoskeleton may change color depending on a louse's surroundings. Brown hair means brown lice. Blond hair means blond lice. This camouflage makes finding lice tricky.

The louse's first body segment is its head. On most insects, bulging eyes dominate the head. However, many lice just have tiny

BUG BYTES

Most insect species have either one or two pairs of wings. However, all phthirapterans lack wings.

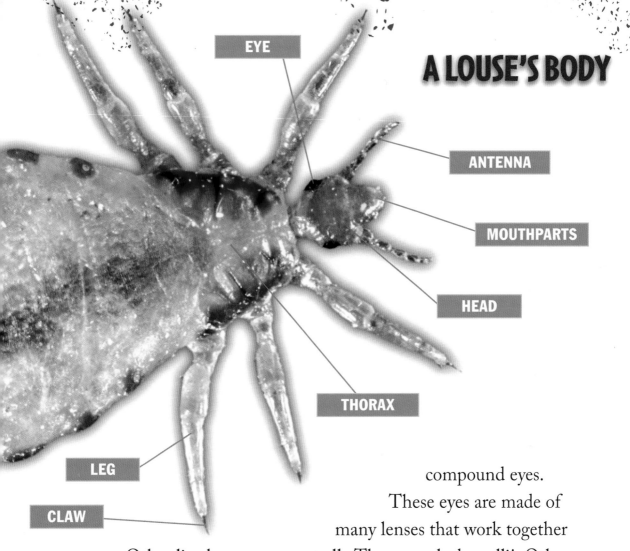

A LOUSE'S BODY

EYE

ANTENNA

MOUTHPARTS

HEAD

THORAX

LEG

CLAW

compound eyes. These eyes are made of many lenses that work together as one. Other lice have no eyes at all. They even lack ocelli! Other insects use these simple eyes to detect light and dark.

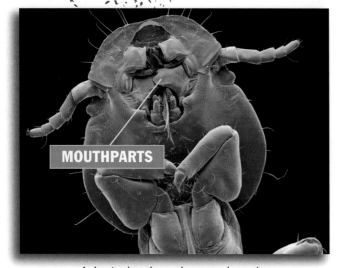

MOUTHPARTS

A chewing louse's mouthparts are located on the underside of its wide head.

The louse's head is small when compared to the rest of its body. The shape depends on the louse's mouthparts and the way it feeds. For example, a sucking louse has a pointed head. Its mouth has sharp stylets for piercing and sucking. A chewing louse has a broad head. Its mouth has jaws for biting.

Both sucking and chewing lice have short antennae. Their antennae are just three to five **segments** long. These function as information devices. They help lice detect food and find their way around.

Beyond the head is the thorax. Six legs connect to this middle segment. Head and body lice have thin legs with small claws. All six legs are about the same length. Their claws grasp the fine hairs on your head.

Crab lice have short legs with heavy claws. The first two legs are slightly smaller than the other four. A crab louse's legs and claws are designed to grasp coarse hair, such as armpit or facial hair.

The abdomen is the louse's largest body **segment**. It is composed of eight to ten smaller segments. In head and body lice, the abdomen is wide at the middle. It tapers toward the thorax and the rear end.

Crab lice are wider than head and body lice. Their name comes from their shape and their heavy claws, which resemble those of ocean crabs.

The Inside Story

Even though a louse is tiny, many things are going on inside its body. There, several systems and **organs** work hard. Together, they keep the louse moving.

Like all living things, a louse needs air. However, it does not breathe the same way you do. Its respiratory system is made up of spiracles and tracheae. Air enters a louse's body through holes called spiracles. Then, tubes called tracheae carry the air to the rest of the body.

A louse has an open circulatory system. This means that blood flows freely through its body. A louse's blood is called hemolymph. A simple tube-shaped heart pumps the hemolymph through the louse's body.

After a louse eats, food passes through its **digestive** system. First, the food enters the louse's foregut. Then, it travels to the midgut. There, the food is digested and absorbed for energy. Finally, waste is released from the hindgut.

A louse has six pairs of spiracles along its abdomen. The thorax has one additional pair of spiracles.

Transformation

There are three stages in the life cycle of a louse. These are egg, nymph, and adult. Going through these stages is called incomplete **metamorphosis**.

A louse takes up to eight weeks to complete the three stages. This life span is determined by several factors. The most important are species and surrounding temperature.

The life cycle begins when a male and female louse mate. Following this, the female louse searches for a place to lay her **fertilized** eggs. The base of a host's strand of hair is a head louse's preferred spot.

The female head louse attaches her eggs, or nits, to the hair. She uses a cementlike substance to create a strong bond. This makes the nits difficult for the host to remove.

Lice lay several nits at a time. These nits are white or gray in color and oval in shape. As you might guess, they are very tiny. Most nits are about the size of the period at the end of this sentence.

BUG BYTES

A head louse's entire life cycle takes place on its host.

A body louse spends most of its life cycle cozy in its host's clothing or bedding. Mating also takes place in these locations.

Nits may be small, but there are a lot of them. This is because the female louse lays eggs every day of her adult life. That really adds up! For example, a single louse lays about seven eggs per day. That means she will lay about 50 eggs in one week. Depending on her **suborder**, a female louse will lay up to 300 nits in her lifetime.

Seven to ten days after being laid, the nits hatch. This is the beginning of the nymphal stage. It lasts one to two weeks. Nymphs look similar to adult lice, but they are smaller and colorless. They are also very hungry. So, nymphs feed many times each day to support their rapid growth.

LIFE CYCLE OF A LOUSE

EGG

NYMPH

Growing so fast means that nymphs outgrow their skin! Underneath, a new, larger skin has formed. This process is called molting. Nymphs molt three times.

After the final molt, nymphs enter the adult stage. Adult lice are bigger than nymphs, but they are still tiny. Fully grown body lice are about one-eighth of an inch (.32 cm) long.

ADULT

Hairy Homes

Different louse species make their homes in different places. Skin, fur, and feathers all make cozy homes for lice. Most species have a specific host they prefer to live on. Of course, all human lice live on or near humans.

Head lice live in a person's hair, usually near the **scalp**. Favorite spots are behind the ears and near the neck. These lice are very dependent **ectoparasites**. They cannot survive more than two days off a host.

Body lice like to hide in clothing, especially in the seams. They also snuggle into blankets, sheets, pillows, and other similar items. These lice survive by crawling onto their hosts for feeding. They cannot survive longer than eight to ten days without a host.

Crab lice live in coarse body hair. Crab lice legs are adapted to moving about in thick, but widely spaced hairs. Like head lice, they cannot survive longer than two days away from a host.

Your head may feel itchy if lice are crawling around on your scalp!

Dinnertime

You read earlier that lice are **ectoparasites**. Ectoparasites feed off of their hosts. Exactly which food source a louse eats depends on its species. For example, the head louse feeds solely on human blood.

A sucking louse keeps its mouthparts within its head when it is not feeding. When it is ready to feed, three stylets extend from the head and pierce the host's skin. One stylet **injects saliva** into the feeding site. This keeps the host's blood from clotting.

Next, sucking begins. Together, two stylets form a tube that channels blood into the louse's body. Other mouthparts called maxillae help by supporting the stylets. The louse feeds until it has had enough to eat. A single feeding can last up to one minute. No wonder lice are such a pain!

BUG BYTES

Only five types of mammals don't get lice. They are anteaters, armadillos, duck-billed platypuses, bats, and whales.

Lice can live up to two days without a blood meal.

Chewing lice have a more varied diet. These lice live on birds and mammals other than humans. Their favorite foods are blood, feathers, skin debris, and **secretions**. However, each species is picky about the type of host it feeds on.

Chewing lice are specially adapted to dine on their feasts. Their mouthparts are able to bite through the thick skin of their hosts. These sharp, pointed mandibles make small wounds in a host's skin and draw out blood to feed on.

Lice will make anyone feel uncomfortable! Most mammals groom each other to remove lice and nits. This is called nit-picking.

No matter which food they eat, lice eat often. They usually dig in for a meal every three to six hours. Since their food source is never far away, frequent snacks are not a problem.

Hog lice are the largest species to infest either farm animals or pets. Females may reach a length of one-quarter of an inch (.64 cm) when fully grown.

Lice and You

Head lice are not dangerous, but they sure can make you miserable! The crawling of these **ectoparasites** can make your head itch. And, some people may have an allergic reaction to louse **saliva**.

This reaction often means itchy **rashes** and hives. Sores can also result from excessive scratching.

Other louse species carry disease. For example, body lice carry a disease called typhus. Typhus causes high fever, headache, and skin rashes. In severe cases, the **infected** person may die. However, typhus is rare in places that are kept clean.

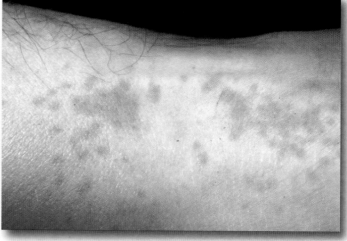

Lice can leave their hosts with many red, uncomfortable bites.

The biggest problem with lice is getting rid of them. Special shampoos and nit combs are helpful against head lice. They remove lice and nits from an **infested** person's head. Taking measures to prevent future infestations slows the overall spread of lice.

An effective nit comb has narrowly placed metal teeth to catch or crush nits. Plastic combs can miss some nits and are not as effective.

FEELING LOUSY?

INTENSE ITCHING IS OFTEN THE FIRST SIGN OF A LICE INFESTATION. FOLLOW THESE STEPS TO TREAT YOUR HEAD LICE.

1) TELL AN ADULT IMMEDIATELY.

2) VISIT YOUR DOCTOR OR THE DRUGSTORE. YOU WILL NEED TO GET A MEDICATED SHAMPOO THAT KILLS LICE.

3) AN ADULT WILL NEED TO USE A NIT COMB TO REMOVE ANY EXISTING NITS. BE SURE TO POP IN A MOVIE FOR THIS PART!

4) CLEAN THE HOUSE! VACUUM THE CARPET AND THE FURNITURE. WASH CLOTHING, BEDDING, AND STUFFED ANIMALS IN HOT WATER. BRUSHES, COMBS, AND HAIR ACCESSORIES SHOULD BE WASHED WITH THE MEDICATED SHAMPOO OR REPLACED.

5) REPEAT TREATMENT IN SEVEN TO TEN DAYS, IF NEEDED.

DON'T WORRY IF YOUR HEAD STILL ITCHES. IT DOESN'T ALWAYS MEAN YOU STILL HAVE LICE. IT MAY JUST TAKE SEVERAL DAYS FOR YOUR SKIN TO HEAL.

Bye-Bye Bites!

Schools often take precautions against lice, especially when equipment must be shared. For example, lining helmets used in gym class can help prevent the transfer of lice.

By now, you know that lice do not jump or fly. These **ectoparasites** use their legs to crawl from host to host. Therefore, lice spread quickly where people or animals are in direct contact.

Direct contact may mean being head-to-head with an **infected** person. Or, it can mean coming in contact with an infected person's personal items. These include combs, brushes, towels, and pillows.

Sharing other personal items such as hats and helmets easily spreads lice as well. Then there are less obvious carriers of lice. Some examples are headphones and earbuds. These easily transport lice, too!

Being aware of the ways lice can travel from one host to the next is important. You may not realize your classmate has lice until these bugs end up on you!

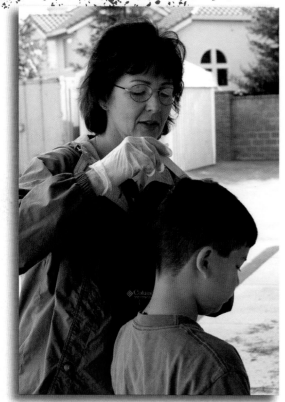

Does your school have a nit-free policy? If so, a student may be sent home if nits are found on his or her head.

Luckily, taking certain measures may help you avoid lice. Don't share hats, earmuffs, or scarves. Use your own brushes, combs, and towels. These are all cozy places for lice to rest between hosts. Try to avoid sharing headphones, earbuds, and athletic headgear. These are less likely carriers, but they may spread lice too.

During the school year, you can have an adult check your hair for lice regularly. If lice are present, the **infestation** can be caught and stopped early. This will save you from a lot of itching and days away from school.

This brings us to an important point. If you end up with lice, don't feel ashamed. After all, lice aren't picky! They will play house on any head they can find. Therefore, having lice is not a sign of poor **hygiene**. So, try to remember that no one should be teased for having lice.

Don't let lice keep you away from your friends. You can make smart choices to prevent these bugs from making you feel lousy!

Glossary

digest - to break down food into substances small enough for the body to absorb. The process of digesting food is carried out by the digestive system.

ectoparasite - a parasite that lives outside its host's body. A parasite is an organism that lives off of another organism of a different species.

entomologist - a scientist who studies insects.

fertilize - to make fertile. Something that is fertile is capable of growing or developing.

hygiene - conditions or practices of cleanliness that are required for good health.

infect - to enter a body and cause disease.

infest - to spread or exist in large numbers so as to cause trouble or harm.

inject - to forcefully introduce a substance into something.

metamorphosis - the process of change in the form and habits of some animals during development from an immature stage to an adult stage.

organ - a part of an animal or a plant that is composed of several kinds of tissues and that performs a specific function. The heart, liver, gallbladder, and intestines are organs of an animal.

rash - a breaking out of the skin with red spots.

saliva - a liquid produced by the body that keeps the mouth moist.

scalp - the part of the head usually covered with hair.

secretion - something that is formed and given off.

segment - any of the parts into which a thing is divided or naturally separates.

suborder - a group of related organisms ranking between an order and a family.

How Do You Say That?

Anoplura - an-uh-PLUR-uh
antennae - an-TEH-nee
camouflage - KA-muh-flahzh
entomologist - ehn-tuh-MAH-luh-jihst
hemolymph - HEE-muh-lihmf
Mallophaga - muh-LAHF-uh-guh
maxillae - mak-SIH-lee
metamorphosis - meh-tuh-MAWR-fuh-suhs
nymph - NIHMF
ocelli - oh-SEH-leye
Phthiraptera - thehr-AHP-tuh-ruh
tracheae - TRAY-kee-ee

Web Sites

To learn more about lice, visit ABDO Publishing Company on the World Wide Web at **www.abdopublishing.com**. Web sites about lice are featured on our Book Links page. These links are routinely monitored and updated to provide the most current information available.

Index